Original title:
Daisy Dreams

Copyright © 2025 Creative Arts Management OÜ
All rights reserved.

Author: Jasper Montgomery
ISBN HARDBACK: 978-1-80566-643-1
ISBN PAPERBACK: 978-1-80566-928-9

Petal Language Unspoken

A budding flower whispers secrets,
Little bugs lend an eager ear.
Each color dances in the sunlight,
While bees giggle, buzzing near.

They laugh at clouds that block the sun,
As petals flutter in the breeze.
A silly game of hide and seek,
With nature's charm that aims to tease.

Dreams Beneath the Blossom Canopy

Under blooms, the world feels silly,
Butterflies wear polka-dot coats.
They waltz about in festive colors,
While frogs recite their funny notes.

Beneath the petals, laughter rings,
As ants march by in marching bands.
Each flower sways with jolly tunes,
While nature plays in playful bands.

Wanderings of a Heart in Bloom

A wandering heart skips through gardens,
Chasing shadows that twist and twirl.
With every step and sudden giggle,
The butterflies chase in a whirl.

Petals blush when the wind declares,
That laughter blooms like wildflower cheer.
A heart that flutters, skips and bounces,
Sings silly songs for all to hear.

Fragments of Joy in Nature's Choir

In nature's choir, the bugs harmonize,
Crickets create their rhythmic beats.
Each blossom sways and tells its tale,
As laughter echoes through the streets.

The leaves join in, a raucous jest,
While squirrels dance in tittering glee.
In every corner, joy is brewing,
A humorous world, wild and free.

Basking in Bloom

In a garden of giggles and glee,
Flowers dance wild, so free,
Bees buzzing like they're in a race,
Tickling petals, oh what a place!

Sunbeams wiggle with joy today,
Chasing shadows that wish they could play,
Frogs in hats croak the silliest tunes,
While butterflies wear their best festooned.

Nature's Canvas of Colors

Colors collide in a vibrant show,
Silly squirrels with paint, on the go,
They splatter their thoughts, oh what a sight,
Making hues laugh in pure delight!

Tulips trumpet their jokes with flair,
Whispers of wind tickle the air,
Laughter echoes down the lanes of green,
Nature's palette, the liveliest scene!

A Tapestry Told in Petals

Petals weave stories, quite absurd,
Roses gossip, shaking their spurred,
Forget-me-nots chuckle in hues of blue,
While sunflowers pose, someone's gotta do!

Marigolds giggle, they sway and twirl,
In a dance that makes the world whirl,
Each bloom a character, quirky and bright,
Creating a tale that ignites pure light.

Flowers Beneath a Starry Veil

Under the stars, tickled by night,
Flowers giggle in soft moonlight,
Crickets join in with their witty tunes,
While sleepy buds bounce in their balloons!

The cosmos winks, caching a joke,
As flowers laugh, the night they invoke,
A raucous party in petals so bright,
Dreaming of candy in the sweet twilight.

Lullabies of the Blooming Heart

In the meadow, cows jump high,
Singing softly, tickle the sky.
Butterflies dance with silly grace,
They giggle, bounce, in a flowery race.

Bumblebees wear tiny hats,
Twirling round with the chitchats.
A ladybug with a tiny drum,
Plays a tune that makes us hum.

Grass blades whisper jokes so sly,
As the ants start to sip their pie.
A flower pot joins the fun,
Tipsy from the morning sun.

In this garden, laughter sings,
Each petal flaps its silly wings.
Close your eyes to the merry art,
And drift with lullabies of the heart.

Beauty in the Floating Breeze

A dandelion wished on a breeze,
Tickled by fluff, it made a tease.
Round and round, with giggles bright,
It tossed its seeds left and right.

Chasing clouds, the shadows play,
Silly critters dance all day.
Squirrels wear sunglasses with flair,
Taking naps on branches, beware!

Flowers joke with scents so sweet,
Making the sun tap its feet.
Wind whispers secrets, long and grand,
As butterflies flutter hand in hand.

In this place where whimsy roams,
Every petal finds a home.
Join the fun, let your heart please,
In beauty found within the breeze.

Whispers of Petal Skies

In the garden, giggles grow,
The sun turns up its golden glow.
Roses telling tales of yore,
While violets peek in to explore.

Bubbles float like fluffy sheep,
Silly secrets, nature's keep.
A butterfly wearing polka dots,
Sips sweet nectar from fancy pots.

Clouds wear socks, a fluffy sight,
While ants hold a dance party at night.
Laughter echoes through the air,
As petals twirl without a care.

So close your eyes and take a ride,
On whispers soft, where dreams abide.
With every laugh, let spirits rise,
In the magic of petal skies.

Sunlit Meadows and Moonlit Wishes

Sunlit meadows, where daisies wink,
Frogs wear crowns, oh, what do you think?
The sun plays tag with shadows near,
While rabbits hop and throw a cheer.

Mice in tuxedos, having fun,
Chasing the shadows as they run.
The grass tickles toes, oh so spry,
As twinkling stars wink in the sky.

Moonlit wishes float like dreams,
With giggling flowers and bright moonbeams.
Toadstools host a fancy bash,
With fireflies lighting up a flash.

In this place, laughter's the tune,
Under the watchful eye of the moon.
So spin around, let joy persist,
In sunlit meadows, where wishes twist.

Fluttering Hues under the Sun

Colors dance in playful glee,
Chasing butterflies, wild and free.
A tickle on the nose, what a tease!
Petals laugh in the gentle breeze.

Bees buzz in a wiggly line,
Painting gardens so divine.
A picnic spread, oats and cheese,
Squirrels plot their nutty schemes!

The sun winks down, oh so sly,
As clouds stroll lazily by.
With laughter echoing through the air,
Nature's jokes without a care.

Under foot, the grass does tickle,
Hopping frogs play their little trickle.
A symphony of wonders sway,
In this laughter-filled cabaret!

A Festival of Color and Light

A carnival of petals burst,
Colors fight for the top, they thirst.
A red rose blushing, bold display,
While yellow pansies prance and play.

Sunshine laughs upon a stage,
Lighting up this floral page.
Each hue's a note, a joyful sound,
In nature's orchestra, they're bound.

Butterflies twirl like dancers bright,
Kissing blooms in morning light.
Laughter swirls with every breeze,
An endless party among the trees.

Bumblebees with tiny hats,
Buzzing like old chitchat cats.
They sip from blooms, then giggle loud,
Joining in this cheerful crowd!

A Mosaic of Nature's Splendor

Picture frames of green and gold,
Nature's palette, daring and bold.
Each flower's shade, a quirky tale,
With blooms jostling, none to pale.

A squirrel slips in shades of brown,
Its antics like a circus clown.
Frogs croak out the evening song,
As crickets chirp, they all belong.

Sunset paints with hues of fire,
In the sky, they jump, aspire.
A giggle from the grass below,
Where bumblebees with socks do show.

The moon arrives, all silvered dreams,
While nature's twilight giggles gleam.
A canvas vast, where wonders meet,
In every corner, smiles repeat!

The Romance of Earth and Sky

Up above, the clouds flirt and tease,
As earth dances swaying trees.
Sunshine sparkles like a wink,
While puddles shimmer, 'What do you think?'

The breeze twirls leaves in a dance,
Giving flowers their happy chance.
Down below, the critters play,
Inventing jokes in their own way.

Rain joins in with splashes bold,
Crafting tales both new and old.
Each drop a giggle, soft and spry,
While rainbow ribbons stretch the sky.

Together they weave a tapestry,
Of nature's winks and harmony.
A love story that never slows,
Between the earth and skies that glow!

The Muse of Nature's Palette

In the garden, colors clash,
A purple cat with a yellow sash.
Bees wear hats, oh what a sight,
While butterflies dance with pure delight.

Sunflowers giggle, tall and proud,
Whispering secrets, laughing loud.
The grass tickles toes, a playful tease,
As ants march forth with utmost ease.

Ladybugs play tag on a leaf,
While worms debate on who's the chief.
Nature's palette, messy and bright,
Painting laughter in morning light.

Where the Wildflowers Roam

Where wildflowers roam, the bees do zoom,
A bumblebee's wiggle fills the room.
Daisies wear crowns made of sun,
And snicker at clouds, just having fun.

A grasshopper hops with a squeaky voice,
In the meadow, it's all a choice.
To dance in the wind or simply nap,
Under the sky's big floppy cap.

A squirrel tells tales of acorn theft,
While roly-poly bugs take a rest.
Here every petal's a soft-spoken joke,
As laughter unfurls in every stroke.

Echoes of Innocence and Grace

In a field where the daisies greet,
A giggly breeze makes them all beat.
The clouds become castles, fluffy and white,
Where marshmallow dreams soar out of sight.

A rabbit who wears glasses reads a book,
While tiny gnomes plan for the next cook.
Nature's wisdom, so playful and bright,
Bringing joy like confetti in flight.

With the sun as a spotlight, the fun unfolds,
Tales of mischief in whispers bold.
Echoes of laughter blink in the grass,
Where innocence flowers as ages pass.

Threads of Hope in Floral Dreams

In a fabric of blooms, laughter weaves,
With petals like socks, and stems like sleeves.
A flower child spins a tale of cheer,
As sunbeams giggle and tickle the ear.

Hopping teacups, spinning like mice,
Swirling wind brings the tastiest spice.
Every sprout shares whimsical plots,
While daisies swap secrets with little knots.

As shadows dance with a fancy flair,
Hope hangs gently in the perfumed air.
Threads of joy twirl in floral themes,
Weaving together our silliest dreams.

Fields of Gold and White

In a field where flowers sway,
A bee decides to take a holiday.
He buzzed about with such great flair,
And wore a tiny, silly chair.

The daisies giggled, tossed their heads,
As he crashed softly on their beds.
A picnic planned – oh what a sight!
A feast with crumbs of pure delight.

He offered pie made of sweet grass,
But someone thought it made him pass.
They laughed and rolled upon the ground,
A joy in laughter all around.

At sunset's glow, they sang a tune,
While dancing 'neath a giant moon.
The flowers swayed to every beat,
Life ain't too bad when you're this sweet.

Garden of Wishes

In a garden filled with silly dreams,
The gnomes plot schemes and plan their beams.
They trade their hats and dance about,
While frogs jump in, and sing their shout.

A toadstool turned into a throne,
Where whispers made of honeycomb.
Each flower told a funny tale,
Of pumpkins that would surely sail.

The butterflies wore capes so bright,
As they buzzed round in pure delight.
They played tag with a bumblebee,
Who just wanted to sip his tea.

By sunset, laughter filled the air,
As everyone forgot their care.
In this whimsy, fun's the rule,
In this garden, oh so cool!

Gentle Breeze and Bloom

Breezes laugh and twirl around,
Tickling petals with a sound.
A ladybug with shades so fine,
Claims she's the queen of the sunshine.

The poppies wear their floppy hats,
While butterflies chat with the cats.
They share old jokes from the past,
And agree that silliness should last.

A windy whisper spills the beans,
Of how grass wears its summer jeans.
And every bloom agrees in glee,
That laughter's best – just let it be!

With every gust, a giggle flows,
As petals dance in funny rows.
In this bright world of cheer and play,
Joy blossoms more than words can say.

Secrets in the Summer Air

Secrets float on summer's breeze,
A playful tune among the trees.
Ants in line with tiny hats,
Marching on to chat with bats.

Each flower wears a unique shade,
Growing silly games they made.
The sunbeams tickle every leaf,
Granting giggles beyond belief.

A curious squirrel spies a joke,
And shares it with a sleepy oak.
The whispers ripple through the grass,
A joyful shout as they all pass.

When night falls down, the stars ignite,
And fireflies join in with their light.
In every secret shared and said,
A world of laughter lies ahead.

Blossoms Beneath a Velvet Sky

In a patch where blossoms meet,
Waltzing petals in a beat,
Giggling gusts that lift the cheer,
They tickle noses, oh so near.

Colors clash in playful sprout,
One pink shy, one too loud bout,
They tumble down in silly flight,
Chasing shadows, laughing bright.

Butterflies with flapping glee,
Join the fun, what a spree!
Pollen-dusted, they all prance,
In this wacky flowery dance.

Stars will twinkle, skies so wide,
As petals giggle, side by side,
Their velvet home, a velvet dream,
With laughter bursting at the seam.

A Tapestry of Soft Hues

In fields of blush and lemon zest,
Petals mock, they laugh, they jest,
Swaths of color spread so bold,
With tales of frolic, still untold.

The lilacs whisper, 'Oh, so bright!'
While violets plot all through the night,
Every hue a silly jest,
A canvas where the blooms can rest.

The marigolds play peek-a-boo,
They prance and dance, a jolly crew,
With gentle sways, their antics tease,
All under ticklish, teasing breeze.

And in this madness, joy persists,
In vibrant swirls, oh, how they twist,
A tapestry of hues misread,
Where laughter sprouts, and dreams are fed.

The Dance of Wildflowers

In fields where wildflowers roam,
They twirl and whirl, they call it home,
A jig, a hop, a sprightly call,
With petals bouncing, oh, they enthrall!

With daisies ducking, 'Now you see!',
And poppies giggling in the spree,
They leap and roll like playful sprites,
In laughter's arms, the day ignites.

The sunbeams join, a wacky friend,
In playful pirouettes that never end,
Together they create a show,
As wildflowers flaunt with teasing flow.

The whispers of the gentle breeze,
Encourage blooms to bend with ease,
And in their merry, wild guitar,
They sing aloud, their tune a star.

Enchanted Fields of Gold

In golden fields, a riot blooms,
Where flowers wiggle, dance, and zoom,
A daffodil trips, a lilac slips,
Their flouncing joy, a comic script.

With every rustle, every sway,
They laugh away the light of day,
A whimsical parade, bright and free,
Together in this jubilee.

Bees are buzzing with a grin,
Finding flowers to buzz within,
They compete for the sweetest cheer,
A nectar chase that brings them near.

As twilight paints the scene in hues,
The flowers giggle, sharing clues,
To dream and twinkle in the fold,
In these enchanted fields of gold.

Fragrant Echoes of Childhood's Lullaby

In the fields where laughter sings,
A butterfly wears silly rings.
With roots that wiggle, grass does tease,
And ants all dance with hapless bees.

The sun, a wink behind the trees,
Whispers jokes on the buzzing breeze.
A kite gets stuck on Grandpa's hat,
While squirrels plot to steal the cat.

Between the blooms, we make a mess,
Building castles from the excess.
The wind it chuckles, wild and bold,
As secrets of the flowers unfold.

So gather round, let's spin and twirl,
While daisies giggle and petals swirl.
With sunshine painted on our cheeks,
We'll chase the joy, for laughter seeks.

Dreamscapes in a Tangle of Blooms

In a garden where gnomes dance,
A worm has taken up romance.
Petals wear the latest trends,
While bees are busy making friends.

A cat in boots struts with a flair,
As daisies giggle, flipping hair.
A rabbit hops, an acrobat,
With carrots flying, on a mat.

We play tag with a sturdy breeze,
And dance with shadows under trees.
A puppet show of flowers bright,
With laughter echoing through the night.

So share a smile, embrace the fun,
As we spin tales 'til the day is done.
With petals twirling, life's a feast,
In this wild world, let happiness be unleashed.

The Serenity of Gentle Gardens

In a nook where starlight beams,
The daisies plot their playful schemes.
Twinkling thoughts with laughter flow,
In a garden, where whimsies grow.

Gnomes are nodding, sipping tea,
While ladybugs hum melodies.
The world forgets its everyday fuss,
As butterflies ride the evening bus.

With every petal, humor found,
As jests are tossed upon the ground.
A crooked fence, a mouse on skate,
Cheering up the flowers' fate.

So let us twirl beneath the moon,
And sing with joy a merry tune.
For in this garden, free and bright,
We'll laugh together, pure delight.

Veils of Color in the Twilight

In the garden where colors collide,
A trio of bugs takes a silly slide.
They giggle and tumble, sharing their schemes,
Dressed in their fanciest nighttime gleams.

As stars blink above with winks of glee,
The flowers sway in hysterics, you see.
A sunflower trips, a rose starts to roll,
While a laughing vine weaves tales to console.

Bees buzzing loudly, a comedic choir,
Thumping their wings like a loud tambourine,
They sway with the rhythm while jamming all night,
Turning the garden into a fun sight!

At dawn, they all pause with a chuckle or two,
For the night's laughter promises to renew.
Together they'll dream of adventures so bright,
In the garden where veils of color ignite.

The Secret Life of Petals

In the secret of petals, whispers abound,
Where soap bubbles fly and laughter is found.
A tulip in pink tells a joke to the bees,
"Why did the blossom refuse to freeze?"

"Oh, because it wanted to bloom with a flair,
And dance with the dew in the light spring air!"
The daisies roll over, unable to bear,
As petals unite in a giggly affair.

The shadows grow long as the jokes go on,
A poppy leaps and begins to yawn.
The violets hum a little tune,
While dandelions twirl, dreaming of the moon.

When night paints the sky with a wink of delight,
The petals conspire in the soft, sleepy light.
Together they whisper of mischief and cheer,
In the secret life of where laughter draws near.

Daylight Dances on Fairytales

Daylight pirouettes, casting spells on the ground,
While critters in stories come twirling around.
A grasshopper leaps with a wink and a smile,
"Let's dance in the sun for a little while!"

A glimmering frog croaks a cheeky refrain,
"Remember last Tuesday? What a day of rain!"
The butterflies flutter with wicked delight,
Planning their antics from morning to night.

The giggles of daisies, a fluttering cheer,
As they cast away worries, embracing some cheer.
With petals and laughter, they spin and they race,
Creating a festival in nature's own space.

As shadows grow long and the sun starts to fade,
Fairytales chuckle at the pranks they have played.
Caught in the revelry, oh, what a sight,
Daylight dances, creating magic tonight!

A Children's Garden of Wonders

In a garden where giggles are planted with care,
Every flower blooms with a spark of a dare.
The roses conspire for a playful exchange,
While the lilacs concoct a prank that's quite strange.

With petals for pillows, the sunflowers leap,
Hosting a party for all—come and reap!
The daisies act silly, strutting about,
Painting the ground with their whimsical shout.

The butterflies flitter, spreading delight,
Telling wild stories of joy in their flight.
Ladybugs laugh at the antics they find,
Creating a whirlwind of fun intertwined.

And as night blankets dreams with a star-dusted cheer,
The children's garden whispers secrets so clear.
In this wonderland, laughter takes wing,
Where every flower dances, and joy's the main thing!

The Language of Blossoms

In the garden where giggles play,
Petals gossip in a funny way.
They tickle the bees with their bright hues,
And dance lightly, sipping morning dews.

With whispers of secrets among the blooms,
Tulips wear hats, and daffodils loom.
Chasing butterflies with a playful shout,
They challenge the clouds to join their bout.

Roses wear crowns, quite proud of their thorns,
While pansies pull pranks, and laughter adorns.
Sunflowers tower, making silly grins,
As daisies trade jokes on the lightest winds.

Starlit Nights and Floral Visions

Under the moon, the flowers chatter,
A comical scene, with laughter that matters.
Petunias pop popcorn, oh what a sight!
While violets dance under soft starlight.

Beneath the glow, the night air is sweet,
Lilacs tell tales that make everyone tweet.
Marigolds juggle, a dazzling display,
While lilies roll laughter in the milky way.

With a rustle and giggle, they stir up the night,
In floral pajamas, what a funny sight!
The garden's a stage for the blooms' grand jest,
In starlit delight, they funnily fest.

A Symphony of Color and Scent

A kazoo of colors in the morning bright,
Sunflowers cheer while the roses take flight.
Daisies in tutus twirl like a dream,
And bumblebees buzz to the floral theme.

In a festival of hues, the laughter is loud,
Forget-me-nots wave in a playful crowd.
Petals like confetti fall from the vine,
As pansies play trumpet, oh how they shine!

The aroma unfolds with a whimsical flair,
Cacti are caught in a soft fragrance snare.
The blooms join the fray, they join in good cheer,
Creating a symphony for all blooms near.

Festooned by Nature's Hand

Nature's jesters in robes of delight,
Waltzing together in morning light.
The tulips join hands, a merry parade,
While daisies play tag, their laughter displayed.

Orchids pull pranks from the branches above,
They flutter and giggle, oh, what a shove!
Each petal a joke, each leaf a refrain,
In the garden of humor, they dance without pain.

With roses as jesters and violets in bloom,
They craft a grand joke to lighten the gloom.
Under the sun, their antics unfold,
And fun is the currency that never grows old.

Reverberations of the Meadow's Breath

In fields where tiny flowers sway,
A bee complains about the hay.
With legs of pollen, he takes flight,
Chasing butterflies, what a sight!

The grass tickles my toes, oh dear!
A giggle escapes, what do I hear?
A rabbit hops with floppy ears,
Spreading joy and bunny cheers!

Clouds float by in silly shapes,
A cat in sunglasses, oh what a gape!
The sun whispers jokes to the trees,
While squirrels laugh with such a tease!

With every gust, the skits unfold,
A snail in slippers, brave and bold.
The world is wacky, laughter's key,
Join the jest, be wild and free!

The Soft Embrace of Earth's Bounty

Beneath the sky of azure hue,
A worm spins tales, quite askew.
He claims he danced with a grand dame,
Who wore a dress of dandelion fame!

A mushroom jokes with passing flies,
His cap a throne, beneath the skies.
They plot a party, wild and grand,
With toadstool seats throughout the land!

The ants parade in perfect lines,
Reciting poems made of twines.
A joke about the sugary crumbs,
Leaves us all with giggly hums!

With every laugh, the daisies sway,
Nature's jesters lead the way.
The earth is filled with chuckles round,
In this green kingdom, joy is found!

Timeless Whimsy of the Fields

In a meadow where laughter's born,
A quirky scarecrow dons a horn.
He sings of corn with such delight,
That even crows stop for the night!

A critter crew sets up a race,
With floppy hats and silly grace.
A hedgehog claims he's quite the sprinter,
While turtles prove they're the real winners!

The flowers giggle as they bloom,
Wiggling like they're in a room.
A breeze whispers secrets, oh so sly,
Tickling petals as they sigh!

With every twist and joyful turn,
Nature's playbook we will learn.
In this landscape, wild and free,
Laughter reigns, come join the spree!

Fluttering Petals and Fanciful Moods

Petals dance upon the breeze,
Telling tales with flickering ease.
A bumblebee wears a tiny hat,
He's off to tea with a fluffy cat!

The butterflies have quite the knack,
For fluttering in a zany pack.
With twirls and spirals, here they go,
A whirl of colors, what a show!

Grasshoppers jump with silly grins,
Challenging the ladybugs to spins.
A conga line of clumsy bugs,
Bringing joy and goofy hugs!

The sun sets low, a golden glow,
Whispers laughter, nice and slow.
In this whimsical living dream,
Life's a stage, we're one big team!

The Sweetness of Blooming Hearts

In gardens where the laughter grows,
A flower wears some silly clothes.
With polka dots and stripes so bright,
It dances through the day and night.

The bees all buzz a merry tune,
While spoons and forks are joined by noon.
A butterfly brings cake to share,
But lands right in a friend's wild hair.

A ladybug hops like a kid,
And leaps right over what she hid.
She's rolling on the petals soft,
With giggles that just can't be stopped.

So here's a treat for all who roam,
In blooms of joy, we find our home.
The sweetness of this playful art,
Is truly found in blooming hearts.

A Canvas of Radiance and Growth

In meadows painted bright and bold,
A canvas where the flowers told.
Each petal stroke, a twisted jest,
As sunbeams shine, they're feeling blessed.

The daisies giggle as they sway,
And tease the clouds that float and play.
With smiles stitched in every hue,
They paint the sky with laughter too.

A dandelion goes for a spin,
While grasshoppers join in the din.
The colors clash, a joyful cheer,
As flowers whisper plans to steer.

A palette of delight unspooled,
Where laughter mingles, joy is ruled.
In playful strokes, we find the worth,
Of laughter woven in the earth.

Fables Woven in the Grass

Beneath the blades, the stories hum,
With critters weaving tales of fun.
The wise old snail moves slow but sly,
While crickets sing their lullabies.

A grasshopper boasts of mighty leaps,
While ants march straight, and never sleep.
Each fable spun in sunlit gleam,
Makes laughter bloom like a sunny dream.

A caterpillar shares a snack,
While all the blooms just chill and crack.
They chat and giggle, safe and sound,
With whispers all around the ground.

So join the fun beneath the sky,
In grassy realms where giggles fly.
Each tale a thread, each laugh a pass,
In fables spun from blades of grass.

Petal-Soft Whispers

In quiet corners, whispers spread,
Soft petal secrets gently fed.
A tulip tells a joke so bright,
And sends the bees into a flight.

The rosebuds snicker at the thyme,
As daffodils create a rhyme.
With giggles dripping from their leaves,
They craft the tales that fun believes.

The breezy breeze joins in the jest,
As blossoms wear their very best.
They twirl and spin, a merry dance,
Encouraging the bees to prance.

So if you stroll where laughter's found,
In petal whispers, joy abounds.
With every bloom, a giggle slips,
In gardens full of friendship's sips.

Soft Shadows on Sunlit Grass

In the field where giggles play,
Bumblebees dance, oh what a day!
Grass tickles toes, a ticklish spree,
As clouds parade, so wild and free.

Silly hats spun round and round,
Laughter echoes with each bound.
Butterflies wear polka dot suits,
While ants march by in fancy boots.

Sunbeams flicker, hide and seek,
A squirrel squeaks, it's far from meek.
Frogs croak songs of sweet delight,
As shadows leap with pure daylight.

Each moment swings with perfect glee,
In this delightful, sun-kissed spree.
With silly tales the heart will clasp,
We lay beneath those soft shadows cast.

The Dreamer's Garden

In a garden where giggles sprout,
Plump tomatoes dance about.
Bees wear crowns and sing a tune,
While carrots hum to the bright moon.

Fairies trade their teasing pleats,
With dandelions as their seats.
Giggling sprouts, so bold and bright,
Play hide and seek in morning light.

The sunflowers stretch up high and wide,
Telling secrets with playful pride.
Gnomes toss hats like frisbees too,
While rabbits race in silly shoes.

In this whimsical patch of earth,
Laughter blooms, oh what it's worth!
For every dream that comes alive,
Within this garden, we all thrive.

Morning Dew and Daydreams

With morning dew that winks and glows,
The sleepy flowers strike their pose.
Frogs wear pajamas, all snug and tight,
While snails are late, they lost the fight.

Puddles form a dancing stage,
Where raindrops leap, and laughs engage.
A squirrel slips on acorn fare,
While giggles float around in air.

Sunshine spills like honey sweet,
As ants create a marching beat.
Bubblegum clouds drift, oh so slow,
Tickling the dreams that ebb and flow.

The morning stretches with a cheer,
As daylight giggles, oh so near.
Majestic moments, silly hues,
In the dance of dreams, we choose.

Echoes of Pastel Skies

In skies of pink where giggles bounce,
Cotton candy clouds surmount.
A painted world, so bright and fair,
With unicorns prancing in the air.

Rainbows twist like silly straws,
While laughter echoes, just because.
Detectives duck in grassy lanes,
Chasing shadows with bright refrains.

The stars come out to play their games,
With twinkling eyes, they call us names.
Moonbeams tease with winks and grins,
Inviting all to join the spins.

So let us dance through pastel dreams,
With giggles bursting at the seams.
As echoes fade in twilight's sigh,
We'll paint our joy across the sky.

Gentle Breezes and Silken Forms

Breezes swirl with playful glee,
Tickling flowers, wild and free.
A butterfly in a waltz, takes flight,
Wearing polka dots, what a sight!

Garden gnomes with painted grins,
Dance around in their old sins.
Who knew they had such slick moves?
Stomping down, the hedgehog grooves!

Sunlight shines, it's quite the show,
Even ants, they sway and flow.
Chasing shadows, bumping heads,
The merrychaos, a buzz instead!

Whispers laugh among the stems,
As chirpy crickets play with hems.
Wind may chuckle, clouds may prance,
In this garden, all take a chance!

Lullabies of Sun-kissed Blooms

Sunbeams dance on petals bright,
Tickling buds, morning light.
Bumblebees hum silly tunes,
While ants march like tiny loons!

Tulips wear their hats so tall,
Making daffodils feel small.
Roses laugh, they have such flair,
How did they get that pink hair?

Glorious shades of mischief bloom,
Buds peek out of mothers' room.
The shady tree, it shakes with cheer,
Roots tapping beats, the flowers cheer!

Jolly clouds float overhead,
Joking with the sleepy bed.
In the garden, joy's a stream,
Where chuckles weave the sweetest dream!

Secrets in the Garden's Heart

In the soil, whispers grow bold,
Worms gossip tales, retold and retold.
Mice chase cheese, as squirrels cheer,
In this garden, joy is near!

The hedges hide a cricket's laugh,
While laughing leaves share their craft.
A lily's hat spins in delight,
Dancing like it's Friday night!

Underneath the vines entwined,
Is a snail, with moves well-defined.
He slides by with a wink and smile,
"Catch me if you can," he'll tease in style!

Tulips gossip, daisies tease,
A raucous shindig in the breeze.
Secrets linger in laughter's part,
In the cozy garden's heart!

Petals Floating on the Stream

Petals sail on water's glide,
Sharing tales of summer's pride.
Jumping fish with glittering skin,
Try to tickle, let the fun begin!

The reeds have rhythm, sway and sway,
As frogs croak jokes in ballet.
Dragonflies prance with a wink and twist,
In this ballet, who'd want to miss?

Down the stream, where giggles flow,
As turtles wear their shells in tow.
One lost shoe? Oh what a laugh,
A frog finds it, now he's the staff!

At sunset's glow, the laughter chills,
As crickets play their nighttime thrills.
With petals floating, laughter's dream,
In this fun, we're a lively team!

Gossamer Threads of Floral Days

In fields of laughter, flowers sway,
With petals tickling, come what may.
Bumblebees buzzing in a silly race,
While butterflies dance with a cheerful face.

A caterpillar giggles as it crawls,
Wearing a crown made of tiny thralls.
Sunshine spills like jelly on the ground,
As ants parade without a sound.

Grasshoppers leap with a comic flair,
Telling jokes on a warm, sweet air.
Together they frolic, a merry crew,
With silly antics that feel so new.

In this garden where laughter grows,
The quirkiest friendships surely flows.
With every bloom that paints the way,
Gossamer threads bind the lighthearted play.

Feelings Chasing the Breezes

Whispers of joy on a warm summer day,
With giggles and surprises tucked away.
A wind that tickles, pulling hearts near,
As kites take flight, spreading just cheer.

Clouds wear hats of cotton candy,
While squirrels debate what's more dandy.
Pine trees sway with a feathery tease,
As laughter drifts on the playful breeze.

Frogs leap around in a chorus of croaks,
Cracking up at their own silly jokes.
Nature's stage always puts on a show,
With each giggle sprouting like daisies that grow.

Chasing feelings like butterflies' flight,
Here in the meadows, everything's bright.
Breezy adventures fill the day's nest,
With whimsical antics, we all feel blessed.

A Gentle Call from the Earth

Under the sun, where daydreams bloom,
Earth calls softly, dispelling the gloom.
A worm with glasses reads a fine book,
While daisies gossip, giving a look.

Ladybugs giggle, sharing a joke,
As the trees sway with a towering poke.
Mice in tuxedos dance in a line,
Charmed by the rhythm of nature's design.

Rain drops like confetti fall from the sky,
Making puddles where tiny feet fly.
The world spins round in a gleeful whirl,
As bees and blooms in delight twirl.

So heed the call, let giggles unfurl,
Beneath a sky with a sparkling pearl.
Join the frolic, hear nature's mirth,
In the joyous song of our lovely Earth.

Constellations of the Meadow

Stars of the meadow twinkle and play,
With daisies glowing at the end of the day.
Fireflies shimmer in a dainty dance,
Inviting the night for a whimsical chance.

Crickets chirp a tune so light,
As shadows twist under the moon's bright sight.
Frolicsome titters from a fox in disguise,
As friendship blooms in the lavender skies.

Mice book a trip on a fluffy white cloud,
While laughter echoes, in joy so loud.
With every twinkle, a joke takes flight,
As constellations welcome the soft night light.

From crook and cranny, the giggles arise,
Painting the horizon with laughter and sighs.
In this dreamy refuge where wonder glows,
The meadow shines bright with its funny shows.

Whispers of the Meadow

In the meadow, grass does giggle,
Flowers shimmy, tease, and wiggle.
Bumblebees buzz with jokes so sweet,
While ladybugs tap dance on tiny feet.

Butterflies flutter, wearing bright socks,
Sipping nectar from curious rocks.
The sun beams down, a playful spray,
While frogs croak haikus in their own way.

A squirrel spins tales from up in a tree,
Of acorn adventures, wild and free.
With every rustle, a laugh to share,
Nature's humor fills the warm air.

A rabbit hops in a top hat so tall,
Whiskers twitching, it's the life of the ball.
With each little hop, giggles abound,
In this meadow where joy can be found.

Petals in the Wind

Petals are tossed, a carnival scene,
They twirl and tumble, a whimsical sheen.
Grasshoppers chuckle at their wild flight,
Skippin' and jumpin' from morn till night.

A breeze blows by with a ticklish touch,
Causing blossoms to giggle so much.
The world is a stage for flowers to play,
In this swirling ballet of green and gray.

Worms in the soil throw their own parade,
Marching to music that never will fade.
They wiggle and jiggle in earthy delight,
Making sure laughter takes off in flight.

Bumblebees buzzing, throwing a feast,
The pollen disco is never the least.
With every beat, joy dances on air,
In the field where fun blooms everywhere.

A Dance Among Blossoms

In a garden where colors collide,
Petals sway gently, side to side.
Squirrels put on their best tap shoes,
As they twirl and whirl, sharing the news.

A clumsy bee buzzes, trips on a stem,
Starts a conga line, just like a gem.
Ladybugs giggle, they waltz in pairs,
Creating a ruckus, forgetting their cares.

Sunflowers spin like ballerinas bright,
With sunflower seeds taking off in flight.
Chirping crickets provide the sound,
As the garden erupts in joy all around.

The moon peeks in, bringing twinkling stars,
Watching the antics of the flowers and bars.
The dance goes on till the break of dawn,
In this festival where fun is drawn.

Sunlit Reverie

Under the sun, the world seems so bright,
Bouncing bunnies bounce with pure delight.
Honeybees chuckle, with wings spread wide,
In a tipsy tango, they take in the ride.

Grass blades whisper, secrets abound,
As ants march in line, to a silly sound.
Worms in the dirt giggle away,
Planning a party for the next sunny day.

A butterfly giggles, wearing a crown,
Slicing through air, it floats without a frown.
The daisies all wink, sharing a laugh,
As clouds drift by, playing a game of half.

In this sunlit world of whimsy and cheer,
Every little moment is precious and dear.
Nature's humor wraps us like a hug,
In a tapestry woven with joy and snug.

The Garden of Lost Fairytales

In a patch where socks found a friend,
A mushroom whispered, 'Let's pretend!'
A rabbit with glasses reads a book,
Tails wagging fiercely, do take a look!

The trees are gossiping, what a sight,
While crickets debate who's the best at flight.
A squirrel with flair designs a hat,
Promises to be a top acrobat!

A fairy tried hard to learn to dance,
But tripped on a weed, oh what a chance!
Petals applaud with a flutter of cheer,
While ants roll their eyes, 'Oh dear, oh dear!'

In this garden where nonsense runs free,
Laughter blooms like a sweet honeybee.
To visit this place, you must wear bright shoes,
And listen for giggles in every hue!

Radiant Echoes in the Grass

The flowers gossip, 'Did you hear?'
A butterfly lost its way in here.
Laughter ricochets from leaf to leaf,
While a ladybug stirs up some mischief.

A worm sings low, a funny old tune,
As frogs jump high and dance by the moon.
With hues so bright and smiles so wide,
Nature's a party, come on, let's glide!

Crickets breakdance, not one step in sync,
Grasshoppers tease them, making them wink.
Glowworms add sparkle, lights dim and sway,
As laughter and melody drift far away.

Oh, what a joy to be lost in this mirth,
A carnival burst right here on Earth!
Chasing echoes in every sweet breeze,
Where silliness blooms with the greatest of ease.

Chasing Shadows in the Sun

Running with shadows that dance on the ground,
With giggles and wiggles, laughter is found.
A cat in a cape tries to lead the way,
While grass blades tickle, inviting to play!

Hats made of leaves, a marvelous sight,
As insects all gather, buzzing with light.
A squirrel with sneakers races the breeze,
While flowers throw confetti, just as you please.

A kite takes flight, tangled in a tree,
A fox stops to chuckle, 'Is that you and me?'
With every shadow that skips with delight,
The sun plays tricks, turning day into night.

At dusk when the sun gets ready to sleep,
The laughter and joy through the garden will creep.
While chasing our shadows, we find endless fun,
Singing in shadows, we all are as one!

Harmonies of Bloom and Breeze

Petals perform a whimsical song,
While bees join in, buzzing along.
A daffodil twirls with grace and flair,
Waving to daisies, 'Don't you dare stare!'

In this concert of color and cheer,
A butterfly sways, its partner not here.
While sentiment drifts on the soft, sweet air,
Crickets on cymbals create quite a scare!

Jubilant roses boast of their hue,
While violets giggle, 'What else can we do?'
The breeze flips the pages of nature's big book,
As saplings join in, with every nook!

All join together in this festive roast,
Celebrating moments we treasure the most.
With laughter in bloom and joy in the trees,
Let's dance to the harmonies of bloom and breeze!

The Language of Flowers

In a garden of whispers, blossoms conspire,
They gossip in breezes, their secrets on fire.
A rose told a lily, 'You dance like a fool,'
While a daffodil chuckled, 'Let's bend every rule.'

The violets giggled, their hue purple-proud,
As daisies debated who'd look best in crowds.
With petals all fluttering, they shared every joke,
While the shy, quiet tulip just silently spoke.

An orchid chimed in, 'Let's throw a grand bash,
With nectar and sunshine — we'll make quite a splash!'
But the sunflower sighed, 'Why the hurry, dear friends?
There's plenty of time till the garden's end.'

So laughter erupted in colors so bright,
Each flower a jester, a wild, joyful sight.

Nightfall in the Wildflower Patch

When the sunlight retreats and shadows creep near,
The flowers start gossiping, chortles you hear.
A marigold mumbled, 'Is it just me, friends?
Or do we all think that the sun's really dense?'

A petunia piped up, 'Tonight, let's be bold —
Let's wear all our scents, let our stories unfold!'
While the moon took a bow, casting silver on blooms,
The daisies were snickering, hiding their grooms.

A wildflower squealed, 'Shh! I think I see stars!'
'What? You think they're just glitter from cosmic bazaars?'
They twinkled in laughter, a night full of glee,
As they danced with the fireflies, wild and carefree.

With petals a-twinkle, they spun in delight,
In a merry bouquet of the long, cheerful night.

Chasing Light Through Petals

With sunbeams in hand and bubbles of air,
The flowers set out, with dreams to declare.
A poppy exclaimed, 'Let's go catch a ray!
If we chase it just right, we might light up the day!'

The violets protested, 'But wait, there's a catch!
What if we end up stuck in a batch?'
But the lilies were laughing, 'We're wild and we're free,
What's life without chasing some light through the spree?'

With petals all fluttering, they dashed to the sun,
They tripped on their roots, oh what funny fun!
A daisy got tangled, a stem-tying jest,
While the tulips just giggled, 'Oh, we're truly blessed!'

As the light danced around, a magical sight,
They twirled in a frenzy, those petals of light.

A Sojourn in Floral Realms

In a magical realm where the flowers converse,
A dandelion winked, 'Let's take a fun burst!'
Exploring the meadows, with whimsy in tow,
They painted the skies with their playful glow.

The petals all fluttered, their laughter a song,
With jokes about ants who marched all day long.
A sunflower grinned, 'Why do we care?
Let's giggle with breezes, shed petals in air!'

In this floral retreat, where whimsy is king,
A rose played the lute, sweet melodies to sing.
While daisies performed, in a spontaneous jest,
Turning the garden into a comedy fest.

With colors so vibrant, and spirits set high,
They shared their secrets with the wind as it sighed.

The Art of Living in Color

In a garden where colors play,
Balloons dance in a bright bouquet,
Jellybeans tumble, oh what a sight,
Sunflowers chuckle in pure delight.

With every hue, a giggle spills,
Sprinkles of joy on hills and thrills,
Lemonade laughs in the warm sunshine,
Life's a canvas, sip and dine.

Crayons argue over who's the best,
While daisies joke, 'We need a rest!'
The painter laughs, not missing a beat,
Splashing the world with colors sweet.

So grab your brush, don't hold it tight,
Let's paint the day, from morn to night,
With whipped cream smiles and rainbow glee,
In the art of life, let's dance and be!

Sunshine Kisses in Verdant Corners

In the corners where shadows hum,
The sun pokes through like a playful drum,
Grass tickles toes, a warm embrace,
While butterflies flutter in a happy race.

Cucumbers tease in their crunchy suits,
Radishes giggle in garden boots,
The scarecrow winks with a straw-tipped hat,
While bees buzz silly and dance like that.

Puddles splash with a cheerful sound,
As ants parade, they march around,
At tea time, spoons stir up delight,
In sunshine kisses, all feels right.

So gather the sunbeams, dance with glee,
In verdant corners, just you and me,
Let laughter bloom like flowers wild,
In a world where joy is garden styled.

Melodies of Flora and Sky

Under azure skies, flowers sing,
Melodies rise on a whispering wing,
Petals twirl to the tune of the breeze,
While grasshoppers hop with mischievous ease.

Clouds whip cream, a fluffy delight,
They giggle softly, a charming sight,
As daisies hum a quirky rhyme,
Nature's band plays in vibrant time.

Bumblebees join in, buzzing away,
On flower tops, they dance and sway,
With honeyed laughs that fill the air,
Their joyful tunes are beyond compare.

So let your heart sway with delight,
In melodies of the day and night,
For every blossom has a song to share,
In life's sweet orchestra, we all can care.

The Poetry of Grounded Dreams

In the soil, where stories grow,
Rooted laughs in the earth's soft glow,
Worms recite verses of underground cheer,
While whimsical thoughts drift crystal clear.

A daffodil dons a comical crown,
As ladybugs plot and won't back down,
With tiny feet, they dance and spin,
In the garden's play, we all win.

The sun dips low, painting skies bright,
As crickets chirp their poems at night,
Fireflies twinkle, writing their tales,
In grounded dreams, laughter prevails.

So gather 'round for a whimsical scheme,
In nature's pages, the wildest dream,
For poetry blooms in every seam,
In the heart of earth, we're all supreme.

Floral Fantasies Unfurled

In a garden so bright, bees buzz around,
Wearing tiny hats, they dance on the ground.
Sunflowers cheer and giggle with glee,
While roses tell jokes as funny as can be.

Pansies wear glasses, looking quite wise,
Talking of weather, and painting the skies.
Tulips in tutus perform a grand show,
As daisies hold hands, stealing the glow.

Butterflies twirl, in sparkles they dive,
Each turn is a treat, keeps laughter alive.
A lily tells secrets, her friends lean in close,
While daisies, in chorus, just giggle the most.

In this world of color, mischief takes flight,
Whimsical blooms make every wrong right.
Under this canopy, mirth's not misplaced,
In floral adventures, there's never a haste.

Under the Blossom's Embrace

Under blossoms that sway, with whimsy they sing,
It's a party of petals, where joy is the king.
A bumblebee stumbles, wearing a frown,
But the daisies all laugh, "Not going to drown!"

A rose whispers gossip, the sun shines in thrall,
While daisies play merry-go-rounds by the wall.
Lilies in laughter, making each bloom sway,
Chasing shadows, as sunlight keeps play.

Join the bouquet of characters bold,
With stories so silly that never grow old.
The vine that keeps twisting has secrets to spill,
Bringing chuckles and snickers that linger until.

Embraced by the blooms, we giggle in glee,
A tapestry woven with laughter, you see.
In this garden of mirth, we dance on the ground,
For the joy that we find in each petal is crowned.

Petal-Covered Pathways

On pathways of petals, we skip with delight,
Wiggling like worms in the soft morning light.
A daffodil shares a tall tale with flair,
While daisies trip lightly, with petals to spare.

The ants throw a picnic, oh, what a scene,
With crumbs of fine bread, it's fit for a queen!
A butterfly joins them, pretending to feast,
While others roll laughing, enjoying the least.

Each flower's a character, humor abounds,
With a giggle parade that knows no bounds.
In petals we blossom, as each joke is shared,
Comedic nature keeps everyone paired.

So skip through this landscape of whimsy and cheer,
Where flowers conspire to spread laughter near.
In petal-covered pathways, we skip, play, and sing,
Finding joy in the little things each bloom can bring.

Enchanted Fields of Serenity

In fields aglow, with laughter so sweet,
Where flowers gossip while tapping their feet.
Bumblebees giggle, wearing shoes of bright gold,
While daisies tease gently, "We're never too old!"

With a wink and a nudge, a tulip ignites,
Sharing puns and laugh-lines on warm, sunny nights.
Ducks parade by in their cute little line,
Chasing after petals like they're sipping on wine.

Breezes whisper jokes while the sun paints the scene,
Each bloom with a chuckle, it's a dream so serene.
Marigolds brag that they shine the most bright,
But they think of the daisies, "They're such a delight!"

In this vibrant tapestry of fun woven tight,
Each laugh in the meadow makes everything right.
With petals as pillows, we giggle and cheer,
In enchanted fields, all worries disappear.

www.ingramcontent.com/pod-product-compliance
Lightning Source LLC
Chambersburg PA
CBHW072139200426
43209CB00051B/147